THE GAY MAN'S MAN'S COOKBOOK

Skylar Blue

Introduction

By Skylar Blue

Every time you open the refrigerator and your cupboards and put together a meal—even something as simple as bread and cheeses and a salad—you are cooking from the gay man within. With this book, I'm hoping to expand your options, share a few of my tricks, and take you to a place where you feel comfortable winging it, even when guests are coming for dinner.

Cooking for my own guests has honed my own ability to cook like a true gay man should. Improvising in the kitchen is partly a question of skills, but it's largely a matter of attitude. You can make the mental shift so that preparing a good home-cooked meal every night isn't a chore but a time to be with your family and friends. Learn how to let them help you, all the while making it fun. There are never enough chances in the fast paced world to connect with friends and family, and cooking gives you an opportunity to do just that. If I pass along one thought—let your family and friends help you make dinner—this book will be a success for me.

While traveling across the country, I get to talk with lots of home cooks. And in every town, from Providence to San Francisco, Ann Arbor to Austin, the same questions come up again and again: Do you cook differently when you're eating with your own boyfriend? What do you do with leftovers? What's the easiest thing you make at home? What do you make when friends come over for dinner?

This book answers those questions while sharing my go with what you've got philosophy. Cooking like a Gay Man means being flexible, creative, and having fun. It means using what's on hand not being afraid to substitute ingredients. Cooking is like sex. If you come at it with the idea that it can be fun and creative, then suddenly it becomes the high point in your day instead of a chore.

My favorite recipes—the ones I make for my own family-- have to be fast and easy. My **Pounded Pancakes** have brilliant color and terrific flavor—and it's a blast to whip up some white filling. You'll find out how to make **Tight Bottom Taco Cups** and **Flamin' Pinwheels**, a savory veggie roll that's great the day after having some **Rainbow Dip**. You're using your leftovers, making a dish that impresses your friends, and, best of all, spending less than five minutes in the kitchen, because your food processor does all the work.

That's the heart of this book. These recipes are simple to make and offer loads of ideas for pulling in leftovers. They'll wow your friends and even get your kids to eat better foods. The book is divided into five sections: Foreplay, Poppers, Twinks, Bear Options and Happy Endings. You can turn to the section that suits your mood, whether you need dinner on the table in twenty minutes or fantastic recipes for a spur of the moment Friday night get-together.

Most of us, especially in gay households, tend to fall back on the same recipes over and over. I've written this book to give you more than new recipes—I want to change your attitude about dinner time. I want to offer ideas that let you come home from a hard day at work and look forward to making dinner, instead of ordering pizza. I want to encourage you to set up adult-time—and some special adult foods—so that when you go back to work, you're rejuvenated. Time is what Americans most lack— and yet the families and friends who cook together and spend time together at the table are healthier and happier and a little gay. Can a cookbook make you a Gay Cook? Let's just say that encouraging you to spend time together in the kitchen and around the table is a great place to start...

So, BON APETITE my gay lovers!

Sincerely,

Skylar Blue

Skylar Blue

TABLE OF CONTENTS

Skylar Blue

FOREPLAY
(APPETIZERS)

Just like sex, every meal needs a starting point. Start off with one of these delectable creations and you'll be sure to get in the mood...

SAUSAGE STUFFING BALLS

1 lb. fresh pork sausage
1-8 oz. pkg. seasoned stuffing mix
¾ C. hot water
½ C. finely chopped onion
½ C. finely chopped celery
1 egg, beaten
½ tsp. baking powder

Combine stiffing mix with hot water. Break sausage into small pieces and add to moistened stuffing mix. Stir in onion, celery, egg, and baking powder until evenly mixed. Shape into balls, using ¼ cup mixture for each ball, and place in baking pan. Cover with foil, securing tightly around pan. Bake in a 325° oven 15 minutes. Remove foil, increase oven temperature to 350° and continue baking 25 minutes or until sausage is done. Makes 18 to 20 balls.

Barebacked-Avocado
(Stuffed Avocado)

2 large avocadoes
5 dried mushrooms, soaked for 30 minutes
¼ lb. shrimp, cooked
3 T. mayonnaise
1 egg yolk
Juice of ½ lemon
1 tsp. curry powder
12 tsp. Tabasco sauce
2 tsp. peanut or vegetable oil
Salt and pepper
Paprika

Halve avocadoes and scoop out half the meat. Sprinkle with lemon to prevent browning. Drain the mushrooms and dice the shrimp. Add to avocado in bowl and dice the shrimp. Add to avocado in bowl with mayonnaise, egg yolk, lemon juice, curry powder, Tabasco, oil, and seasonings. Mix together and fill avocadoes. Sprinkle with paprika. Serve at once. Serves 4.

Asian Mini-Balls
(Chocolate Snowballs)

2/3 C. butter
1 C. confectionary's sugar
3 T. Cocoa
1 tsp. vanilla
½ C. firmly chopped nuts
½ C. quick rolled oats

Mix above ingredients well—Roll into balls, then roll in white or colored coconut. Refrigerate for 4 hours.

Chubby Chaser Cheddar Cheese Soup

1 ½ C. diced potatoes
1 C. chopped onion
1 tsp. salt
2 beef bouillon cubes
2 C. water
1 C. beer
¼ lb. grated Cheddar cheese

Combine first 5 ingredients in a covered pan and simmer until vegetables and tender., about 10 minutes. Pour into blender and puree. Return to pan and add cheese, stirring over low heat until cheese melts. Gradually whisk in the beer and stir until it is well mixed into the cheese. Serve hot. Yields 4 to 6 servings.

Jock Beef Skewers

1 ½ lbs flank steak
MEAT MARINADE:
3 T. light soy sauce
3 T. dark soy sauce
2 ½ T. sugar
4 T/ sherry
2 cloves garlic, minced
3 ½ T fresh ginger, minced
4 T. sesame oil

Unroll the entire steak. Trim off excess fat. Cut steak into 1/8" slices across the grain. Marinade for 4 hours or overnight in refrigerator. String sliced beef on bamboo skewers like ribbon candy. Barbecue over charcoal or in oven broiler for just a few minutes. Turn once to brown both sides.

Yields 4 servings.

DDF - Ham Sticks

4 slices ham (about ½" thick)
2 tsp. soy sauce
2 tsp. sesame seeds, plus additional seeds for sprinkling
4 T. peanut or vegetable oil
Salt and pepper

Cut the ham into 2x1" strips. Turn in mixture of soy sauce, sesame seeds, and seasonings. In skillet, heat oil; drain; sprinkle with additional seeds and serve. Makes about 24 strips.

NOTE: A good way to use leftover ham. You can either serve the ham with toothpicks or make very small sandwiches using thin whole wheat bread.

Tight Bottom Taco Cups

1 bag Tostitos® Scoops!®
1 can refried beans
1/2 lb cooked taco seasoned meat
1 C. shredded cheddar
1 C. salsa
1/2 C. sour cream
1/2 C. sliced black olives

Set chips on a large platter and layer with beans, meat, cheddar, salsa, sour cream and black olives

Macho Deviled Eggs

6 large eggs - hard boiled and peeled
1/3 C. mayonnaise
1 tsp. prepared mustard
Salt to taste
Paprika if desired

Cut each egg in half lengthwise and remove yolks to a bowl.

Mash yolks well and blend with mayo, mustard and salt.

Fill whites with yolk mixture using a spoon, a pastry bag or a plastic bag with the corner snipped off.

Sprinkle with Paprika, if desired and refrigerate, covered, until serving time.

Slow-Roasted Cherry Tomato Bruschetta

3 pints cherry tomatoes
1 T. extra-virgin olive oil
3 cloves minced garlic
½ tsp salt
½ tsp ground pepper
¼ C. sliced fresh basil
1 T. red-wine vinegar
14 slices baguette, toasted

Preheat oven to 325°F.

Toss tomatoes with oil, garlic, salt and pepper. Place on a baking sheet and roast until broken down, 45 to 55 minutes.

Combine the roasted tomatoes with basil and vinegar.

Top baguette slices with the roasted tomato mixture. Garnish with anchovy fillets, Kalamata olives or sliced fresh basil.

Rainbow Dip
(Cheesy Spinach and Artichoke)

8 oz. cream cheese - softened
10 oz. chopped spinach - thawed and squeezed of excess water
1 (14 ounce) can artichoke hearts - drained well
1/2 C. green onion, tops only - divided
1/2 C. Parmesan cheese - divided
1 C. mozzarella - divided
1/4 C. mayonnaise
2 cloves garlic - minced

Heat oven to 350 degrees F and set aside 1/4 cup green onion, 1/4 cup Mozzarella cheese and 1/4 cup Parmesan cheese.

Blend together remaining ingredients and pour into an 8x8 greased baking dish.

Top with the onions and cheese that has been set aside and bake for 20 minutes until bubbling and cheese is melted.

Serve hot with crackers.

Rainbow Dip Bread Bowl
(Spinach Dip in Bread Bowl)

1 T. olive oil
1 onion, chopped
1 1/2 tsp. kosher salt
2 cloves garlic, minced
1 C. plain Greek 2 percent yogurt (if you can't get the
Greek kind, then drain regular plain yogurt in a coffee-
filter-lined sieve for a couple of hours so it gets nice and
thick)
1/2 C. cottage cheese
1/2 C. mayonnaise
1- 10-oz. box frozen spinach, thawed, drained, then
squeezed dry by the handful
1 (8-ounce) can water chestnuts, coarsely chopped
Black pepper
Lemon
1 round loaf bakery wheat bread, the top sliced off and
diced into 1-inch cubes, and the inside torn out and cut or
pulled into pieces.

Heat oil in a wide frying pan over medium heat and sauté onion with salt, stirring frequently, until it's very nicely browned, about 15 minutes. Add garlic right at the end, and sauté, stirring, another minute before turning off the heat.

Meanwhile, in a food processor whir together yogurt, cottage cheese, and mayonnaise until smooth. Add the slightly cooled onion mixture and spinach, and whir until nearly smooth.

Scrape dip into a bowl, stir in water chestnuts, then season to taste with pepper, a squeeze or two of lemon juice, and more salt.

Scoop into the hollowed loaf or — good-bye germs! — individually hollowed-out rolls, and serve with raw veggies and the bread innards, or try Homemade Pita Chips or Homemade Tortilla Chips

Hey, Hey, HEY, Dumplings

2 C. (packed) sliced Chinese cabbage
1/2 lb. ground pork
2 tsp. soy sauce
1 T. dry sherry
2 tsp. cornstarch
1 1/2 tsp. minced, peeled gingerroot
1 green onion, minced
36 (3/4 12-ounce package) wonton-skin wrappers*, 3 1/2" by 3 1/4"
1 large egg white, beaten
Soy Dipping Sauce (below)
Green onions for garnish

Prepare filling: In 2-quart saucepan over high heat, in 1 inch boiling water, heat cabbage to boiling. Cook cabbage 1 minute; drain. Immediately run cold water over cabbage to cool. With hands, squeeze as much water out of cabbage as possible.

Finely chop cabbage. Squeeze liquid from chopped cabbage; place in medium bowl. Stir in pork, soy sauce, sherry, cornstarch, ginger, and green onion.

Arrange half of wonton-skin wrappers on large sheet of waxed paper. With pastry brush, brush each wrapper lightly with egg white. Spoon 1 rounded teaspoon filling onto center of each wonton wrapper. Bring opposite corners of wonton wrapper up over filling; pinch and pleat edges together to seal in filling. Repeat with remaining wonton wrappers, egg white, and filling

In deep 12-inch skillet over high heat, heat 1/2 inch water to boiling. Place all dumplings, pleated edges up, in one layer in skillet. Stir gently with spoon or heat-proof spatula to prevent dumplings from sticking to bottom of skillet. Heat dumplings to boiling. Reduce heat to low; cover and simmer 5 minutes or until dumplings are cooked through.

Meanwhile, prepare Soy Dipping Sauce: In small serving bowl, mix 1/4 cup soy sauce, 1/4 cup seasoned rice vinegar or white wine vinegar, 2 tablespoons angel-hair-thin strips peeled gingerroot.

Makes about 1/2 cup sauce.

Flamin' Pinwheels
(Veggie Pinwheels)

8 oz. regular or low-fat cream cheese, softened
1 T. finely chopped fresh dill
1 T. lemon juice
1/2 tsp. paprika
1 garlic clove, minced
Salt and pepper to taste
1/2 C. grated carrot
1/2 C. finely chopped red bell pepper
1/2 C. tiny frozen peas, thawed
1 C. fresh broccoli, steamed, cooled, and chopped
6 (6- to 8-inch) white or whole wheat flour tortillas

In a bowl, blend together the cream cheese, dill, lemon juice, paprika, garlic, and salt and pepper using a rubber spatula. Gently fold in the vegetables.

Spread some of this mixture across each tortilla (1/4 cup for 6-inch tortillas, 1/2 cup for 8-inch), leaving roughly 1 inch bare at the top. Then, starting from the bottom, roll the tortillas up tightly (the filling will now spread right up to the bare edge).

If you're making these ahead, wrap each tortilla in plastic wrap and refrigerate. When you're ready to serve, slice each tortilla crosswise into as many pinwheels as you like.

POPPERS
(BREAKFAST)

Poppers are needed to give you a boost and stamina and with this selection from The Gay Man's kitchen, you'll be sure to open right up and take it all in.

POUNDED PANCAKES

PANCAKES:

1 C. sifted flour
¼ tsp. baking powder
1 egg
½ C. milk
½ C. water
2 T. vegetable oil
2 T. butter

Sift flour and salt in a bowl. Beat in egg, milk and water until smooth, then stir in oil. Chill 2 hours. Beat again. The mixture should be like cream. If too thick, add milk. Melt a little butter in a 7" skillet. When it bubbles, pour in just enough batter to thinly coat bottom, about 1 tablespoon. Cool just until set and lightly browned, then turn over. Stack while preparing the filling.

Makes about 12 pancakes.

Pounded Pancake FILLING:

¼ C. Swiss cheese, grated
1 C. Parmesan cheese, grated
1 egg, beaten
¼ C. milk
¼ tsp. white pepper
¼ tsp. nutmeg
3 T. butter
½ C. light cream

Mix together Swiss cheese, ½ cup Parmesan cheese, the egg, milk, pepper and nutmeg. Place a heaping tablespoon on each pancake and roll up. Arrange in a single layer in a buttered shallow baking dish. Dot with butter. Sprinkle with remaining cheese and add the cream. Bake in preheated 350° oven for 15 minutes or until browned.

1st Timer Muffins

1 3/4 C. all-purpose flour
1 tsp. baking soda
¼ tsp. salt
4 ripe bananas
1/3 C. softened unsalted butter
3/4 C. white sugar
1 egg
1 tsp. vanilla extract
1/4 C. whiskey (such as Jack Daniel's®)
1/2 C. unsweetened flaked coconut
1 C. mini chocolate chips

Preheat an oven to 350 degrees F. Grease 12 muffin cups, or line with paper muffin liners. Whisk the flour, baking soda, and salt together in a bowl; set aside.

Beat the bananas, butter, and sugar with an electric mixer in a large bowl until smooth. Beat in the egg, vanilla extract, and whiskey. Mix in the flour mixture until just incorporated.

Fold in the coconut and chocolate chips, mixing just enough to evenly combine. Pour into muffin pan.

Bake in the preheated oven until a toothpick inserted into the center comes out clean, about 25 minutes. Cool in the pans for 10 minutes before removing to cool completely on a wire rack.

Grinder Granola

8 C. rolled oats
1 1/2 C. wheat germ
1 1/2 C. oat bran
1 C. sunflower seeds
1 C. finely chopped almonds
1 C. finely chopped pecans
1 C. finely chopped walnuts
1 1/2 tsp. salt
1/2 C. brown sugar
1/4 C. maple syrup
3/4 C. honey
1 C. vegetable oil
1 T. ground cinnamon
1 T. vanilla extract
2 C/ raisins or sweetened dried cranberries

Preheat the oven to 325 degrees F (165 degrees C). Line two large baking sheets with parchment or aluminum foil.

Combine the oats, wheat germ, oat bran, sunflower seeds, almonds, pecans, and walnuts in a large bowl. Stir together the salt, brown sugar, maple syrup, honey, oil, cinnamon, and vanilla in a saucepan. Bring to a boil over medium heat, then pour over the dry ingredients, and stir to coat. Spread the mixture out evenly on the baking sheets.

Bake in the preheated oven until crispy and toasted, about 20 minutes. Stir once halfway through. Cool, and then stir in the raisins or cranberries before storing in an airtight container.

Puerto Rican Papi Breakfast Burritos

8 (8-inch) flour tortillas
8 ounces bulk pork sausage
2 large baking potatoes, peeled and shredded
1 medium-size green bell pepper, chopped
1/2 cup chopped onion
8 large eggs
2 tablespoons butter or margarine, melted
1/2 teaspoon salt
1/4 teaspoon freshly ground pepper
2 cups (8-ounces) shredded cheddar cheese
Taco sauce for accompaniment

Wrap tortillas in aluminum foil and bake at 350°F for 12 to 15 minutes or until heated.

Brown sausage in skillet, stirring until it crumbles; remove sausage from skillet and set aside.

Drain the drippings and add the potato, green pepper, and onion to skillet; cook over medium heat, stirring occasionally, until tender. Add the butter, when melted add the eggs, salt and pepper; cook, stirring occasionally, until eggs are firm, but still moist. Remove from heat; stir in reserved sausage.

Work with 1 tortilla at a time, keeping remaining tortillas covered and warm. Place about 3/4 cup egg mixture onto each tortilla. Roll up tightly, and place, seam-side down, in a lightly greased 13 x 9 x 2-inch baking dish. Cover with aluminum foil and bake at 375°F for 10 minutes. Remove cover and sprinkle with cheese, cover, and bake an additional 5 minutes or until cheese melts. Serve with taco sauce.

Makes 8 servings.

Morning Slammer

1 large egg, beaten
1/4 cup milk
1/8 teaspoon vanilla extract
2 tablespoons creamy or crunchy peanut butter
1 tablespoon jelly
2 slices whole wheat bread
1 tablespoon butter

In a shallow bowl or pie pan, beat egg, milk and vanilla
until blended; set aside.
Spread peanut butter and jelly on bread to make a
sandwich.

Melt butter in a skillet over medium-high heat; dip
sandwich into egg mixture then grill until golden brown
on both sides.

Serve immediately.

Makes 8 servings.

Raspberry Croissant Melts

4 croissants
1/4 cup raspberry preserves
4 (1-ounce) slices Muenster cheese
1 tablespoon butter

Slice croissants in half and evenly spread the preserves on the cut sides of the croissants. Place a slice of cheese over the preserves on the croissant bottoms and replace the tops.

Melt the butter in a large skillet over medium-low heat and place the croissants upside down in the skillet. Grill until golden and the cheese has melted, about 3 minutes on each side.

Makes 4 servings.

Golden Sunrise French Toast

2 large eggs
1 (12-ounce) can Evaporated Low fat 2% Milk
2 teaspoons vanilla extract
2 tablespoons granulated sugar
1 tablespoon plus 1 1/2 teaspoons all-purpose flour
1/4 teaspoon salt
8 to 10 slices (3/4-inch-thick) firm, day-old French bread
Unsalted butter
Maple syrup
Fresh seasonal berries or sliced fruit

Heat large skillet over medium heat for 3 to 4 minutes.

Beat eggs in shallow pan or large pie plate; whisk in
evaporated milk and vanilla extract. Whisk in sugar, flour
and salt. Add several slices of bread; soak without over
saturating.

Swirl 1 tablespoon butter in hot skillet. Remove bread
from batter, allowing excess batter to drip off; transfer
prepared bread to skillet in single layer. Cook for 2
minutes or until golden brown. Turn over; cook for an
additional 2 minutes or until golden. Serve immediately
with syrup and berries. Continue with remaining bread

slices, adding 1 tablespoon butter to skillet for each new batch.

Lemon Breakfast Parfaits

3/4 cup fat-free milk
Dash salt
1/3 cup couscous
1/2 cup lemon low-fat yogurt
1/2 cup reduced-calorie dairy sour cream
1 tablespoon honey
1/4 teaspoon finely shredded lemon peel
3 cups assorted fruit, such as sliced strawberries, kiwifruit, nectarine, or star fruit; and/or blueberries or raspberries
Chopped crystallized ginger (optional)
Fresh mint (optional)

In a medium saucepan bring the milk and salt to boiling; stir in the couscous. Simmer, covered, for 1 minute. Remove from heat; let stand for 5 minutes. Stir with a fork until fluffy. Cool.

In a small bowl combine the yogurt, sour cream, honey, and lemon peel; stir into the couscous. In another bowl combine desired fruit.

To serve, divide half of the fruit mixture among 6 parfait glasses. Spoon couscous mixture over fruit; top with remaining fruit. If desired, garnish with chopped crystallized ginger and mint.

Makes 6 servings.

Apples 'N Berries Breakfast Crisp

Filling:
4 cups thinly sliced peeled apples (about 4 medium)
2 cups fresh or frozen blueberries or mixed berries
1/2 cup brown sugar, firmly packed
1/4 cup frozen orange juice concentrate, thawed
2 tablespoons all-purpose flour
1 teaspoon ground cinnamon

Topping:
1 cup quick or old fashioned oats
1/2 cup brown sugar, firmly packed
1/3 cup butter, melted
2 tablespoons all-purpose flour

Vanilla yogurt for accompaniment (optional)
Heat oven to 350°F. Grease an 8-inch square glass baking dish with vegetable shortening.
For Filling: Combine all ingredients in large bowl; stirring to coat fruit evenly; spoon into baking dish.
For Topping: Combine all ingredients in medium bowl, mixing until crumbly. Sprinkle evenly over fruit.
Bake 30 to 35 minutes or until apples are tender.

Serve warm topped with vanilla yogurt, if desired.
Makes 9 servings.

Wide-Set Va-Jay-Jay Pita Breakfast

1 pita bread, cut in half
2 eggs
salt and pepper to taste
1/2 C. cooked and diced potatoes

Preheat oven to 350 degrees F. Place pita bread in oven
to warm.

Heat a medium skillet over high heat. Coat with cooking
spray. Add potatoes and sauté until lightly browned,
about 5 minutes. Reduce heat to medium and add eggs.
Mix gently until eggs are firm, about 45 seconds. Season
with salt and pepper. Remove pita from oven. Stuff pita
with potato and egg mixture. Eat immediately.

Skylar Blue

TWINKS
(LIGHT MAIN COURSES)

Mmmm, the favorite guilty pleasure of many; Twinks, are a breed all of their own. Some hot, some shy, and a few are here for anything ... this grouping is sure to fill your need for something willing to satisfy all your dreams.

Bossy Bottom Chicken
(Basil Chicken Over Angel Hair)

1- 8 oz. package angel hair pasta
2 tsp. olive oil
½ C. finely chopped onion
1- clove garlic
2 ½ C. chopped tomatoes
2 C. boneless chicken
¼ C. chopped fresh basil
½ tsp. salt
1/8 tsp. hot pepper sauce
¼ C. Parmesan cheese

In a large pot of salted boiling water, cook angel hair pasta until it is aldente, about 8 – 10 minutes. Drain, and set aside.

In a large skillet, heat oil over medium-high heat. Sauté the onions and garlic. Stir in the tomatoes, chicken, basil, salt and hot pepper sauce. Reduce heat to medium, and cover skillet. Simmer for about 5 minutes, stirring frequently, until mixture is hot and tomatoes are soft. Toss sauce with hot cooked angle hart pasta to coat. Serve with Parmesan cheese.

You've Got Crabs

1- 7oz can crabmeat
½ onion
1 tsp. soy sauce
1 egg
¼ C. cooked rice
1 T. cornstarch mixed with 1 T. water
Salt and pepper
2 C. peanut or vegetable oil

Mince crabmeat and onion. Place in bowl and add soy sauce. Beat egg. Add to bowl. Add rice, cornstarch mixture and seasoning. Mix together and form into balls, golf ball size. Heat oil in skillet. Deep-fry the balls until golden brown. Drain and serve in chafing dish with toothpicks. Leftover chicken or meat can be used in place of the crabmeat. Sprinkle the balls with a little chopped parsley for decoration. Makes about 24.

BROWN TROUT

4 fresh trout, dressed
1C. vinegar
3C. water
2 sprigs parsley
2 T. chopped onion
1 bay leaf
½ tsp salt
Pepper

Wash trout under cold running water. Form each fish into a ring by tying head to tail with a strong thread. Bring remaining ingredients to a boil in a kettle. Plunge in trout and simmer 4 to 6 minutes, just long enough to cook. Drain well. Serve garnished with parsley and lemon wedges, and with boiled potatoes covered with melted butter-parsley sauce or plain melted butter.

Serves 4.

NOTE: The gay way of preparing trout is to marinate or cook it in a vinegar solution, which turns the skin to a vivid blue.

ROSEBUD SALAD

2 C. raw cauliflower
½ C. pitted ripe olives, chopped
1/3 C. green pepper, chopped fine
¼ C. pimiento, chopped
3 T. onion, chopped
DRESSING:
4 ½ T. olive oil
1 ½ T. lemon juice
1 ½ T. wine vinegar
1 tsp. salt
¼ tsp. sugar
Dash pepper

In medium bowl, combine cauliflower, olives, green pepper, pimiento and onion. Make the dressing in a small bowl by combining oil, lemon juice, vinegar, salt, sugar, and pepper; beat with rotary beater until well blended. Pour over cauliflower mixture. Refrigerate, covered, until well chilled, at least 1 hour. To serve, spoon salad into bowl, or if desired, arrange on lettuce on individual salad plates.

Makes 4 servings.

Boy Hole Stew

1/3 C. flour
1 tsp. salt
Dash of pepper
1 ½ lbs lean lamb, cut in 1" cubes
3 C. water
3 onions, sliced
4 potatoes, cubed
1 turnip, diced
5 carrots, quartered
1 ½ C. frozen peas
¼ C. water

Combine flour, salt and pepper. Coat meat well. Save remaining flour. Brown meat in hot fat in a 4-quart saucepan. Add water and cover. Simmer until meat is tender, about 1 ½ hours. Add onions, potatoes, turnip and carrots. Cover, simmer 15 minutes. Add peas. Cover and simmer until vegetables are tender. Blend water and remaining flour. Add to stew. Stir. Cook until think.

Serves 6.

"BJ" Cucumber Salad

3 large cucumbers
2 tsp. salt
1 ½ C/ thick sour cream
3 T. vinegar
½ tsp. black pepper
¾ tsp. chopped chives or dill

Peel and wash cucumbers; slice very thin. Place in china bowl. Sprinkle with salt. Let stand for 1 hour or longer. Squeeze cucumbers dry. Combine remaining ingredients and pour over the cucumbers. Mix well and serve. Makes 4 to 6 servings.

Slapped Ham Meat Loaf

1 lb. ground ham
2 lbs. ground pork
1 egg, beaten
1 C. bread crumbs
½ C. milk
3 T. tomato soup
Paprika
Salt
1 C. brown sugar
¼ C. water
¼ C. vinegar

Combine ham, pork, egg, bread crumbs, soup, paprika
and salt. Mix well and form in loaf. Put onion slices on
top. Bring brown sugar, water, and vinegar to a boil and
pour over top. Bake at 325° for 2 hours.

MUSTARD SAUCE:

½ C. tomato soup
½ C. prepared salad mustard
½ C. vinegar
½ C. sugar
3 beaten egg yolks

Cook over low heat, stirring constantly. This can be used as the glaze for the Slapped Ham Meat Loaf.

Vagina and Salmon Salad
(Tuna Fish & Salmon Salad)

1- 7oz. can salmon
1- 7oz. can tuna fish
1 Spanish onion
½ tsp. salt
2 tsp. soy sauce
2 tsp. peanut or vegetable oil
1 tsp. vinegar
2 slices ginger, chopped

Put the salmon and tuna with juice in a large bowl. Chop onion fine. Add salt. Mix together soy sauce, oil, and vinegar. Chop ginger and add to bowl. Pour soy sauce dressing over fish mixture and toss. Serves 3 to 4.

Mail-Order Slut
(Stir-fried Beef)

1-1/2 pound sirloin steak
2 teaspoons vegetable oil
1 clove garlic, minced
1 teaspoon vinegar
1/8 teaspoon salt
1/8 teaspoon pepper
2 large onions, sliced
1 large tomato, sliced
3 cups boiled potatoes, diced

Trim fat from steak and cut into small, thin pieces.

In a large skillet, heat oil and sauté garlic until garlic is golden. Add steak, vinegar, salt, and pepper. Cook for 6 minutes, stirring beef until brown.

Add onion and tomato. Cook until onion is transparent.

Serving suggestion: Boiled potatoes and white rice.

6 servings; Serving size: 1-1/4 cup

Smalls Chicken & Fruit Salad

1/4 cup reduced-fat sour cream
3 tablespoons fruit-flavored vinegar
1 1/2 teaspoons poppy seeds
1/4 teaspoon salt
Freshly ground pepper, to taste
8 cups mixed salad greens
2 cups sliced cooked chicken breast
2 cups chopped melon, such as cantaloupe and/or honeydew
1/4 cup chopped walnuts, toasted
1/4 cup crumbled feta cheese

Whisk sour cream, vinegar, sugar, poppy seeds, salt and pepper in a large bowl until smooth. Reserve 1/4 cup of the dressing in a small bowl. Add the mixed greens to the large bowl and toss to coat. Divide among 4 plates and top with chicken, melon, walnuts and feta. Drizzle each portion with 1 tablespoon of the reserved dressing.

NOTE:

Tips: To poach chicken breast: Place boneless, skinless chicken breasts in a medium skillet or saucepan and add lightly salted water to cover; bring to a boil. Cover, reduce heat to low and simmer gently until chicken is cooked through and no longer pink in the middle, 10 to 12 minutes.

To toast chopped or sliced nuts, heat a small dry skillet over medium-low heat. Add nuts and cook, stirring, until lightly browned and fragrant, 2 to 3 minutes.

Almond-&-Lemon-Crusted Fish with Spinach

Zest and juice of 1 lemon, divided
1/2 cup sliced almonds, coarsely chopped
1 tablespoon finely chopped fresh dill or 1 teaspoon dried
1 tablespoon plus 2 teaspoons extra-virgin olive oil, divided
1 teaspoon kosher salt, divided
Freshly ground pepper to taste
1 1/4 pounds Pacific cod or halibut (see Note), cut into 4 portions
4 teaspoons Dijon mustard
2 cloves garlic, slivered
1 pound baby spinach
Lemon wedges for garnish

Preheat oven to 400°F. Coat a rimmed baking sheet with cooking spray.

Combine lemon zest, almonds, dill, 1 tablespoon oil, 1/2 teaspoon salt and pepper in a small bowl. Place fish on the prepared baking sheet and spread each portion with 1 teaspoon mustard. Divide the almond mixture among the portions, pressing it onto the mustard.

Bake the fish until opaque in the center, about 7 to 9 minutes, depending on thickness.

Meanwhile, heat the remaining 2 teaspoons oil in a Dutch oven over medium heat. Add garlic and cook, stirring, until fragrant but not brown, about 30 seconds. Stir in spinach, lemon juice and the remaining 1/2 teaspoon salt; season with pepper. Cook, stirring often, until the spinach is just wilted, 2 to 4 minutes. Cover to keep warm. Serve the fish with the spinach and lemon wedges, if desired

Serves 4.

Smooth Porker
(Chicken)

1 cup reduced-sodium chicken broth
3 tablespoons reduced-sodium soy sauce
2 tablespoons molasses, preferably blackstrap
1/4 teaspoon freshly ground pepper
5 teaspoons cornstarch
2 tablespoons canola oil, divided
1 pound pork tenderloin, trimmed, halved lengthwise and
cut into 1/4-inch-thick pieces
1 medium onion, slivered
1 medium red bell pepper, thinly sliced
3 cups bean sprouts
1 tablespoon minced fresh ginger

Combine broth, soy sauce, molasses and pepper in a
medium bowl. Transfer 2 tablespoons of the mixture to a
small bowl; stir in cornstarch until combined. Set aside.

Heat 1 tablespoon oil in a large nonstick skillet over
medium heat. Add pork and cook, stirring frequently, until
most of the pink is gone, 2 to 3 minutes. Transfer to a
plate.

Increase heat to medium-high. Add the remaining 1 tablespoon oil, onion, bell pepper, sprouts and ginger and cook for 3 minutes. Pour in the broth mixture and bring to a boil. Cook, stirring, for 3 minutes. Reduce heat to medium; add the reserved cornstarch mixture and pork (and any accumulated juice) and cook, stirring, until slightly thickened, about 1 minute.

4 servings, 1 cup each

Chicken with Sugar Snap Peas & Spring Herbs

1 cup reduced-sodium chicken broth
1 teaspoon Dijon mustard
1/2 teaspoon salt
Freshly ground pepper to taste
2 teaspoons plus 1 tablespoon flour, divided
1 pound thin-sliced chicken breast cutlets
1 tablespoon extra-virgin olive oil
8 ounces sugar snap peas, cut in half (2 cups)
1 14-ounce can quartered artichoke hearts, rinsed
1/4 cup sprouted beans, (see Note), optional
3 tablespoons minced fresh herbs, such as chives, tarragon or dill
2 teaspoons champagne vinegar, or white-wine vinegar

Whisk broth, mustard, salt, pepper and 2 teaspoons flour in a small bowl until smooth.

Sprinkle both sides of the chicken with the remaining 1 tablespoon flour. Heat oil in a large nonstick skillet over medium-high heat. Cook the chicken in two batches, adjusting heat as necessary to prevent burning, until golden, about 2 minutes per side. Transfer the chicken to a plate; tent with foil to keep warm.

Stir the broth mixture and add to the pan along with snap peas, artichoke hearts and sprouted beans (if using). Bring to a simmer, stirring constantly. Reduce heat to maintain a gentle simmer and cook until the snap peas are tender-crisp, 3 to 5 minutes.

Return the chicken to the pan, nestling it into the vegetables, and simmer until heated through, 1 to 2 minutes. Remove from heat; stir in herbs and vinegar.

Salmon Roasted with Tomatoes & Olives

2 pounds ripe plum tomatoes, stem ends trimmed, cut into thin wedges
1/2 medium onion, peeled and cut into thin wedges
2 strips orange zest, cut into thin slivers
2 cloves garlic, minced
1 T. extra-virgin olive oil
1/3 C. pitted Kalamata olives, coarsely chopped
1 T. chopped fresh rosemary
1/4 tsp. salt
Freshly ground pepper, to taste
1 1/4 lbs. salmon fillet, (about 1 1/2 inches thick), skin removed (see Tip), cut into 4 portions

Preheat oven to 400°F. Combine tomatoes, onion, orange zest and garlic in a large roasting pan or on a large baking sheet with sides. Drizzle with oil and toss to coat.
Roast, uncovered, stirring occasionally, until the tomatoes and onion are tender and beginning to brown on the edges, about 45 minutes. Remove pan from the oven. Increase oven temperature to 450°.
Add olives and rosemary to the pan; season with salt and pepper. Clear four spaces in the pan and place a salmon piece in each. Spoon some of the tomato mixture on top. Roast until the salmon is opaque in the center, 10 to 15 minutes, depending on the thickness.

BEAR OPTIONS
(MEATY MAN COURSES)

You big muscular meat fiends needs something to keep you going in all that Cave action. Bear Options gives you just that while taking it hard, hung, and sometimes a bit hairy.

Hard-Man Baked Beans

2 cups navy beans
1 ½ quarts cold water
¼ lb pork (salt pork)
4 T. molasses
1 tsp. salt
½ tsp. mustard
Hot water.

Wash beans. Add water, boil 2 minutes, then remove from heat and let soak 1 hour. Or add water and let soak overnight in cool place.

Boil soaked beans gently in same water for 45 minutes or until they begin to soften.

Make cut through rind of pork about ½ inch apart. Put half the pork in a bean pot or glass baking dish. Add beans and the rest of the pork.

Mix molasses, salt and mustard with a little hot water, pour over the beans, and add enough hot water to cover beans. Cover: bake at 250° for 7-8 hours. Add a little hot water from time to time during the last hour of baking.

Minute-Man Steaks w/Butter Sauce

1 T. salad oil
2 Beef cubed steaks
Garlic salt
2 T. butter or margarine
1 T. Lemon Juice
1 T. Worcestershire sauce
½ tsp. chives
¼ tsp dry mustard

Heat oil in 1/8" skillet; cook steaks over medium heat until brown, about 4 minutes on each side. Season with garlic salt. Remove steaks from skillet, drain fat and keep warm. Melt butter in same skillet, stirring in remaining ingredients and heat. Place steaks on plate, pour butter mixture onto each side.

Double-Penetrated Hamburger Pie

2 ½ lb ground beef
¼ C. chopped onion
¼ tsp. salt
Black pepper
1 can cut green beans, drained
½ can condensed tomato soup or 1 C. ketchup
1 C. mashed potatoes
3 T. shredded natural cheddar cheese

Heat oven to 350°. In 8" skillet cook and stir meat and onions until meat is brown and onion is tender. Stir in seasoning, beans, and soup. Pour into ungreased 1-quart casserole dish. Bake until mixture is hot and top is slightly brown. About 30 minutes. Makes 4 servings.

Lubed-up Lasagna

1lb. lasagna noodles, cooked
2-16 oz. jars meatless sauce
2 C. large curd cottage cheese
½ C. grated Parmesan cheese
¾ C. chopped onion
1 lb. mozzarella cheese
1 clove garlic
2 tsp salt
2 eggs, beaten
2 lbs. ground beef
1 tsp. Italian seasoning

Cook ground beef, garlic and onion in a large heavy saucepan until beef is done. Add sauce, salt and seasoning and mix well. Simmer gently 15 minutes. Combine eggs and cottage cheese. Grease a 12x9 1/2x2 1/2" baking pan and arrange first layer of lasagna and then alternating layers of the remaining ingredients, ending with a top layer of sauce. Sprinkle with Parmesan cheese. Bake at 350° for about 15 minutes.

Hung Italian Chicken Cacciatore

2 ½ to 3 lb. frying chicken, cut up
1 env. Seasoned coating mix for chicken (Italian flavor)
1-8 oz. can stewed tomatoes
1-8oz. can tomato sauce
½ C. dry white wine
¼ tsp. rosemary leaves

Coat chicken with coating mix as directed on package, reserving and leftover crumbs. Arrange chicken in single layer in a shallow baking dish. Bake at 400° for about 40 minutes, or until well browned. Meanwhile, combine stewed tomatoes, tomato sauce, wine, rosemary and reserved crumbs in a saucepan. Bring to a boil. Spoon sauce over part of each chicken piece in the pan. (Do not cover pieces completely.) Continue baking 10 to 15 minutes longer or until chicken is tender. Makes 4 servings.

Hung Sausage Casserole

6 Link Sausages (Hot or Sweet)
2-4 Green peppers
6-10 Potatoes, quartered
2 Large Onions, diced

Cut green peppers in strips, put in casserole pan. Add potatoes, and onions, laying sausage on top and fill with water. Fill until everything is covered. Bake at 400° for 2-3 hours. Keep covered while baking.

Slurped Spaghetti

5 pounds ground beef
5 medium onions, chopped
1 bunch celery, chopped
8 (14.5 ounce) cans diced tomatoes, drained
2 (6 ounce) cans tomato paste
1 cup Worcestershire sauce
1/2 cup sugar
4 tablespoons salt
4 pounds uncooked spaghetti

In two large Dutch ovens or soup kettles, cook the beef, onions and celery over medium heat until meat is no longer pink; drain. Stir in the tomatoes, tomato paste, Worcestershire sauce, sugar and salt. Bring to a boil. Reduce heat; cover and simmer for 1 hour, stirring occasionally.

Cook spaghetti according to package directions; drain. Serve with meat sauce.

"Boo-boo's" Mac and Cheese

1 (8 ounce) package elbow macaroni
1 (8 ounce) package shredded sharp Cheddar cheese
1 (12 ounce) container small curd cottage cheese
1 (8 ounce) container sour cream
1/4 cup grated Parmesan cheese
salt and pepper to taste
1 cup dry bread crumbs
1/4 cup butter, melted

Preheat oven to 350 degrees F. Bring a large pot of lightly salted water to a boil, add pasta, and cook until done; drain.

In 9x13 inch baking dish, stir together macaroni, shredded Cheddar cheese, cottage cheese, sour cream, Parmesan cheese, salt and pepper. In a small bowl, mix together bread crumbs and melted butter. Sprinkle topping over macaroni mixture.

Bake 30 to 35 minutes, or until top is golden.

Pot O' Meat

1 pound fully cooked kielbasa or smoked Polish sausage, cut into 1/2-inch slices
1 pound skinless, boneless chicken breast halves - cubed
1 large onion, chopped
1/2 cup chopped celery
1/2 cup chopped green pepper
4 garlic cloves, minced
2 tablespoons butter
1 (14.5 ounce) can diced tomatoes, un-drained
1 (6 ounce) can tomato paste
1/2 teaspoon hot pepper sauce
1/4 teaspoon cayenne pepper
1/8 teaspoon garlic powder
1/8 teaspoon white pepper
1/8 teaspoon pepper
1/2 pound uncooked medium shrimp, peeled and deveined
Hot cooked rice

In a Dutch oven or large saucepan, sauté the sausage, chicken, onion, celery, green pepper and garlic in butter until chicken is browned. Stir in the tomatoes, tomato paste and seasonings. Bring to a boil. Reduce heat; cover and simmer for 6-8 minutes or until chicken is no longer pink.

Stir in shrimp; cover and simmer for 4 minutes or until shrimp turn pink. Serve over rice if desired; or cool, cover and freeze for up to 2 months.

Piggy's Pork Chops

2 teaspoons salt
1 teaspoon dried sage
1 teaspoon ground black pepper
6 center cut bone-in pork chops
2 tablespoons butter
1 cup water
2 cubes beef bouillon

Combine the salt, sage and black pepper in a small bowl and rub on both sides of the chops. Melt the butter or margarine in a large skillet over medium high heat and sauté the chops for 5 minutes per side, or until well browned.

Meanwhile, in a separate small saucepan over high heat, combine the water and the bouillon and stir until bouillon dissolves. Add this to the chops, reduce heat to low, cover and simmer chops for 45 minutes.

Awesome (One-Night-Stand) Pot Roast

2 (10.75 ounce) cans condensed cream of mushroom soup
1 (1 ounce) package dry onion soup mix
1 1/4 cups water
5 1/2 pounds pot roast

In a slow cooker, mix cream of mushroom soup, dry onion soup mix and water. Place pot roast in slow cooker and coat with soup mixture.

Cook on High setting for 3 to 4 hours, or on Low setting for 8 to 9 hours.

HAPPY ENDINGS
(DELECTABLE DESSERTS)

Damn, that was a good meal. Now to end with what it's all about ... a Happy Ending. Choose from your fetishes, deep dark pleasures or something you just want to try.
Try it, we dare you.

Double Stuffed Cookies

2 C. sugar
1 C. butter, melted
4 T. anise seed
4 T. anisette or other anise-flavored liqueur
3 T. whiskey, or 2 tsp. vanilla and 2 T. water
2 C. almonds, chopped coarse
6 eggs
5 ½ C. unsalted flour
1 T. baking powder

Mix sugar with butter, anise seed, anise liqueur, whiskey and nuts. Beat in the egg. Mix flour with baking powder and stir into the sugar mixture; blend well. Cover and chill 2 to 3 hours. Directly on greased baking sheets (without sides), shape dough with your hands to form flat loaves that are about ½" thick and 2" wide and as long as the baking sheet. Place no more than 2 loaves, parallel and well part, on a pan. Bake in a 375° oven for 20 minutes.

Remove from oven and let the loaves cool on pans until you can touch them, then cut in diagonal slices that are about ½" to ¾" thick. Lay slices on cut sides, close together on the baking sheets, and return to the 375° oven for 15 minutes more or until toasted. Cool on wire racks and store in airtight containers. Makes about 9 dozen.

Of-Age Cookies

1 C. butter, room temp.
1 C. sugar
2 eggs, well beaten
2 C. flour
½ C. Irish whiskey
¼ C. raisins, blanched and chopped
½ C. almonds
¼ C. chopped candied citron

Preheat oven to 375°. Cream butter with sugar until light and fluffy. Beat in the eggs until well blended. Add the flour and Irish whiskey and beat until smooth. Add the fruit and nuts and mix well. Drop from a spoon onto a greased cookie sheet and bake for 6 to 8 minutes. Remove from sheet while warm and cool on a rack. Makes about 2 dozen cookies.

Dingle-berry Apple Pie

1 egg
¾ C. sugar
1 tsp. vanilla
¼ tsp salt
½ C. flour
½ C. chopped nuts
1 C. diced apples

With a wooden spoon, mix the ingredients in the order given, folding in the nuts and apples last. Put the mixture in an 8" greased pie pan. Bake at 350° for 30 minutes. Serve the pie warm or cold. Makes 6 servings.

Man Berries in Cream

3 pt. boxes strawberries
2 T. lemon juice
¾ C. sugar
Red food coloring
2 envs. unflavored gelatin
½ C. cold water
2. C heavy cream
Fresh mint springs.

Wash strawberries and drain well. Crush half the strawberries with a potato masher or blend for 1 minute in electric blender. In a large bowl, combine crushed strawberries, lemon juice, sugar, and a few drops of coloring. Stir until blended. Sprinkle gelatin in small saucepan over cold water to soften.

Heat over low, stirring constantly, until dissolved. Stir gelatin into strawberry mixture. Place bowl in larger bowl of ice and water. Chill, stirring once in a while, until mixture thickens and mounds slightly. Beat cream, in a large bowl, until stiff. Fold chilled gelatin mixture into cream. Pour into a 2-quart shallow glass serving bowl. Refrigerate about 4 hours. Decorate with springs of mint.

Makes 6 servings.

Rim Job: Cherry Torte

1 qt. large black cherries
½ C. kirsch
4 C. confectioner's sugar
3 T. cornstarch
½ lb butter or margarine
3 egg yolks
2-8" sponge cake layers, 1" thick
1 C. finely shaved bitter-sweet chocolate

Wash cherries; remove stems and seeds. Mix kirsch and 1 cup sugar, and pour over fruit in bowl. Let stand at least 2 hours, and then heat to boiling. Mix cornstarch with 2 tablespoons cherry juice and stir into cherries. Cook and stir until slightly thickened. Remove from heat and let cool.

This should be like a thin jelly. Beat butter and remaining sugar smoothly together. Beat egg yolks into this and continue beating until mixture is light and fluffy. Place layer of cake on plate; make border around the edge with butter mixture and spread some butter cream in circle in center of the cake. Spread cooled cherry mixture between butter cream border and center. Place second layer on top; press down just enough to make layers stick with remaining butter cream. Sprinkle top with shaves chocolate. Makes 6 to 8 servings.

420 No-Bake Cookies

2 C. sugar
½ C. softened butter or margarine
½ C. milk
4 tsp. cocoa

Combine all ingredients into medium saucepan. Bring all ingredients to a boil. Pour into an 8"cake pan, cool, cut into squares

Foot Fetish Delight
(Ladyfingers)

4 eggs, separated
2/3 cup white sugar
7/8 cup all-purpose flour
1/2 teaspoon baking powder

Preheat oven to 400 degrees F. Line two 17 x 12 inch baking sheets with baking parchment. Fit large pastry bag with a plain 1/2 inch round tube.

Place egg whites in bowl and beat on high until soft peaks start to form. Slowly add 2 tablespoons of the sugar and continue beating until stiff and glossy. In another bowl beat egg yolks and remaining sugar. Whip until thick and very pale in color.

Sift flour and baking powder together on a sheet of wax paper. Fold half the egg whites into the egg yolk mixture. Fold in flour, and then add the remaining egg whites. Transfer mixture to pastry bag and pipe out onto prepared baking sheet. Bake 8 minutes.

Asian Wang
(Tiramisu)

6 egg yolks
3/4 C. white sugar
2/3 C. milk
1 1/4 C. heavy cream
½ tsp. vanilla extract
1 lb. mascarpone cheese
1/4 C. strong brewed coffee, room temperature
2 T. rum
2 (3 ounce) packages ladyfinger cookies
1 T. unsweetened cocoa powder

In a medium saucepan, whisk together egg yolks and sugar until well blended. Whisk in milk and cook over medium heat, stirring constantly, until mixture boils. Boil gently for 1 minute, remove from heat and allow to cool slightly. Cover tightly and chill in refrigerator 1 hour.

In a medium bowl, beat cream with vanilla until stiff peaks form. Whisk mascarpone into yolk mixture until smooth.

In a small bowl, combine coffee and rum. Split ladyfingers in half lengthwise and drizzle with coffee mixture.

Arrange half of soaked ladyfingers in bottom of a 7x11 inch dish. Spread half of mascarpone mixture over ladyfingers, then half of whipped cream over that. Repeat layers and sprinkle with cocoa. Cover and refrigerate 4 to 6 hours, until set.

Automatic Orgasm

1 (18.25 ounce) package chocolate cake mix
1 C. Reduced Fat Sour Cream
1 pkg. (4 serving size) JELL-O Chocolate Instant Pudding
4 eggs
1/2 C. oil
1/2 C. water
3 C. thawed COOL WHIP Whipped Topping, divided
1 (8 ounce) package Semi-Sweet Chocolate
1 1/2 C. raspberries

Preheat oven to 350 degrees F. Lightly grease 12-cup fluted tube pan or 10-inch tube pan. Beat all ingredients except whipped topping, chocolate and raspberries in large bowl with electric mixer on low speed just until moistened. Beat on medium speed 2 minutes scraping bowl occasionally. Pour into prepared pan.

Bake 50 minutes to 1 hour or until wooden toothpick inserted near center comes out clean. Cool in pan 10 minutes. Loosen cake from side of pan with knife or metal spatula and gently remove cake. Cool cake completely on wire rack. Place on serving plate.

Reserve 2 Tbsp. of the whipped topping. Microwave remaining whipped topping and chocolate in microwaveable bowl on HIGH 1-1/2 to 2 minutes or until chocolate is completely melted and mixture is well blended, stirring after each min. Drizzle over cake. Immediately drop reserved whipped topping, by scant teaspoonfuls, around top of cake; create star shape by drawing wooden toothpick through middle several times. Spoon raspberries into center of cake. Store leftover cake in refrigerator.

Cheesy Nacho Bake

1 lb. lean ground beef
1 (14.5 ounce) can diced tomatoes, un-drained
1/4 C. water
1 (1.25 ounce) package taco seasoning mix
3/4 C. Sour Cream, divided
6 oz. tortilla chips
1 1/2 C. Shredded Mild Cheddar Cheese
1 green onion, sliced

Heat oven to 350 degrees F.

Brown meat in large skillet; drain. Return meat to skillet. Add tomatoes, water and seasoning mix; stir. Cook 10 minute, stirring occasionally. Stir in 1/4 cup sour cream.

Place half the chips in 13x9-inch baking dish; cover with layers of half each of the meat mixture and cheese. Repeat layers.

Bake 20 minute or until heated through. Top with onions and remaining sour cream.

Dessert Crepes

4 eggs, lightly beaten
1 1/3 cups milk
2 tablespoons butter, melted
1 cup all-purpose flour
2 tablespoons white sugar
1/2 teaspoon salt

In large bowl, whisk together eggs, milk, melted butter, flour sugar and salt until smooth.

Heat a medium-sized skillet or crepe pan over medium heat. Grease pan with a small amount of butter or oil applied with a brush or paper towel. Using a serving spoon or small ladle, spoon about 3 tablespoons crepe batter into hot pan, tilting the pan so that bottom surface is evenly coated. Cook over medium heat, 1 to 2 minutes on a side, or until golden brown. Serve immediately.

Fudge Packer

16 ounces semisweet chocolate
1 (14 ounce) can sweetened condensed milk
2 teaspoons vanilla extract
1 1/2 C. chopped walnuts

Line an 8x8 inch square dish with aluminum foil.

Chop chocolate and place in a large, microwave safe bowl with condensed milk. Microwave on high, stirring once or twice until chocolate is soft, 2 to 3 minutes. Remove from oven and stir until completely smooth. Stir in vanilla and walnuts. Spread in prepared pan.

Refrigerate 2 hours, until firm. Cut into squares.

INDEX

Foreplay (Appetizers)

Asian Mini-Balls 4
Barebacked-Avocado.........3
Chubby Chaser Cheddar
Cheese Soup.......................5
DDF - Ham Sticks................7
Flamin' Pinwheels............16
Hey, Hey, HEY,
Dumplings.........................14
Jock Beef Skewers..............6
Macho Deviled Eggs..........9
Rainbow Dip 11
Rainbow Dip
Bread Bowl........................12
SAUSAGE
STUFFING BALLS.................2
Slow-Roasted Cherry
Tomato Bruschetta..........10
Tight Bottom
Taco Cups............................8

Poppers (Breakfast)

1st Timer
Muffins..............................20
Apples 'N Berries
Breakfast Crisp.................30
Golden Sunrise
French Toast.....................28
Grinder
Granola..............................22
Lemon Breakfast
Parfaits..............................29
Morning Slammer............26
Pounded Pancakes..........18
Puerto Rican Papi
Breakfast Burritos............24
Raspberry
Croissant Melts................27
Wide-Set
Va-Jay-Jay Pita
Breakfast...........................31

Twinks
(Light Main Courses)

Almond-&-Lemon-
Crusted Fish
with Spinach....................46
"BJ" Cucumber Salad.......39
Bossy Bottom
Chicken..............................34
Boy Hole Stew..................38
BROWN TROUT................36
Chicken with
Sugar Snap Peas...............50
Mail-Order Slut................43
ROSEBUD SALAD.............37
Salmon Roasted with
Tomatoes & Olives.........52
Slapped Ham
Meat Loaf.........................40
Smalls Chicken
& Fruit Salad....................44
Smooth
Porker...............................48
Vagina and
Salmon Salad...................42
You've Got Crabs.............35

Bear Options
(Meaty Man Courses)

Awesome
(One-Night-Stand)
Pot Roast.........................64
"Boo-boo's"
Mac and Cheese...........61
Double-Penetrated
Hamburger Pie...............56
Hard-Man
Baked Beans...................54
Hung Italian
Chicken Cacciatore.........58
Hung Sausage
Casserole.........................59
Lubed-up Lasagna...........57
Minute-Man Steaks
w/Butter Sauce...............55
Piggy's Pork Chops...........63
Pot O' Meat......................62
Slurped Spaghetti...........60

Happy Endings
(Detectable Desserts)

16097892R00051

Made in the USA
Lexington, KY
05 July 2012